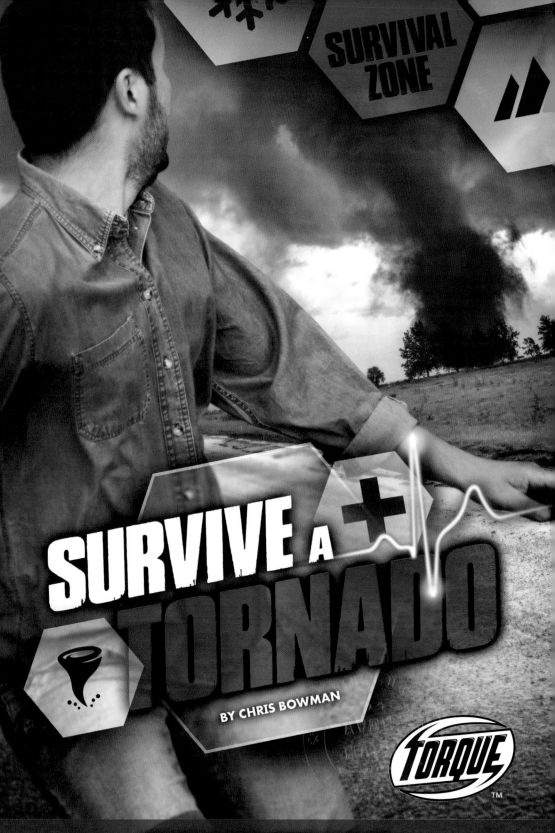

SURVIVAL ZONE

SURVIVE A TORNADO

BY CHRIS BOWMAN

TORQUE™

BELLWETHER MEDIA · MINNEAPOLIS, MN

Are you ready to take it to the extreme? Torque books thrust you into the action-packed world of sports, vehicles, mystery, and adventure. These books may include dirt, smoke, fire, and chilling tales. **WARNING**: read at your own risk.

This edition first published in 2017 by Bellwether Media, Inc.

Library of Congress Cataloging-in-Publication Data

Names: Bowman, Chris, 1990- author.
Title: Survive a Tornado / by Chris Bowman.
Description: Minneapolis, MN : Bellwether Media, Inc., [2017] | Series:
   Torque: Survival Zone | Includes bibliographical references and index. |
   Audience: 007–012.
Identifiers: LCCN 2015051373 | ISBN 9781626174443 (hardcover : alk.
   paper)
Subjects: LCSH: Tornadoes–Juvenile literature. | Severe storms–Juvenile
   literature.
Classification: LCC QC955.2 .B69 2017 | DDC 613.6/9–dc23
LC record available at https://lccn.loc.gov/2015051373

Printed in the United States of America, North Mankato, MN.

TABLE OF CONTENTS

A VIOLENT STORM

May 20, 2013 is a clear morning in Moore, Oklahoma. Students are happy to see the sun after recent stormy weather.

Around midday, clouds form over the town. A nearby siren soon goes off. A tornado has touched down in the area! Students, including 11-year-old Alexander Ghassimi, file into the hallways. They have practiced this during tornado safety drills.

"We looked up and the whole ceiling was gone."
-Alexander Ghassimi

"It almost looked like *The Wizard of Oz*: just a bunch of papers and books above us."
-Alexander Ghassimi

Plaza Towers Elementary
Moore, Oklahoma

This tornado is especially strong. Teachers rush students into the bathrooms and cover them as the storm hits. The roof flies off the building!

Soon, the tornado is over. Much of the school is destroyed. Some of the students do not make it out. But Alexander and hundreds of other students and teachers survive the storm.

WHIRLING WINDSTORMS

Tornadoes are storms with strong, rotating winds. They can pick up houses, tear off roofs, and throw **debris** at high speeds.

Tornadoes are unpredictable. They can last a few seconds or an hour. Their paths stretch from 5 yards (4.6 meters) to more than 1 mile (1.6 kilometers) wide. Paths may be short or more than 100 miles (160 kilometers) long!

HOW TORNADOES DEVELOP

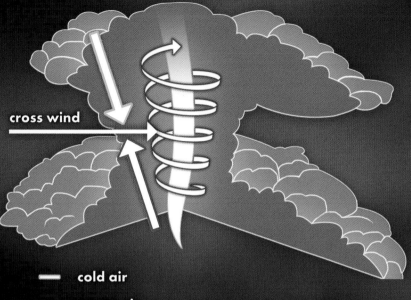

cross wind

— cold air

— warm air

STORMING IN

The strongest tornadoes have spinning winds of more than 300 miles (483 kilometers) per hour!

9

Tornadoes can form at any time. Most occur in spring and summer. They often happen in the afternoon. Tornadoes usually form out of thunderstorms.

Meteorologists use radar to predict when tornadoes will develop. They issue watches and warnings. Many cities have tornado sirens to warn citizens when one is near. The Enhanced Fujita Scale ranks the storm's strength.

THE ENHANCED FUJITA SCALE

The Enhanced Fujita Scale ranks tornadoes based on their wind speed and the damage they have done.

EF-0:
65-85 mph (105-137 km/h)

EF-1:
86-110 mph (138-177 km/h)

EF-2:
111-135 mph (178-217 km/h)

EF-3:
136-165 mph (218-266 km/h)

EF-4:
166-200 mph (267-322 km/h)

EF-5:
200+ mph (322+ km/h)

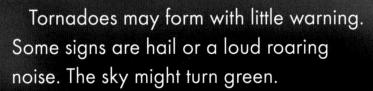

CAUGHT OUTSIDE

Tornadoes may form with little warning. Some signs are hail or a loud roaring noise. The sky might turn green.

If you are caught outside, the safest option is to find a sturdy shelter. If none are nearby, lay facedown in a ditch or on low ground. Keep away from trees and other big objects. Protect your head and neck with your arms.

TYPES OF TORNADOES

cone tornado

rope tornado

stovepipe tornado

wedge tornado

BY ANY OTHER NAME

Tornadoes are also called twisters, whirlwinds, and cyclones.

Cars and **mobile homes** are unsafe during tornadoes. The wind can pick them up. If a tornado is near, get out of the car and crawl into a ditch. Avoid stopping the car under bridges. Wind travels faster there.

TAKING BY STORM

Each year, more than 1,000 tornadoes are reported in the United States.

It might be possible to escape a tornado if it is far away. Drive to a shelter as quickly as possible.

STAYING INDOORS

The safest place to be during a tornado is in a **bunker**. Many buildings in **Tornado Alley** have these storm shelters.

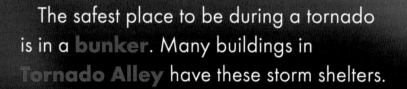

HEADS UP

Wearing a bicycle or other sports helmet can help keep you safe during a tornado.

If there is no bunker nearby, get to the lowest level of the building. Basements are best. Small rooms without windows such as closets or bathrooms are other safe options.

TORNADO ALLEY

Tornado Alley range =

Underneath stairwells can also be good places to take cover. Once in a safe room, kneel on the floor and cover your head. Use a mattress or table to protect from flying debris.

If you are in a big or unfamiliar building, stay calm. Watch to see what others are doing. Then move quickly to a more protected area.

AFTER THE TORNADO

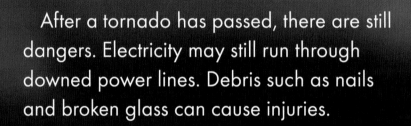

After a tornado has passed, there are still dangers. Electricity may still run through downed power lines. Debris such as nails and broken glass can cause injuries.

Food and clean water might be tough to find. Always keep an emergency supply kit in the safest room in the house. Preparing for the unexpected can make a big difference after a tornado!

EMERGENCY KIT LIST

dry or canned food	bottled water	can opener	emergency radio	flashlight	extra batteries	first aid kit

medications	clothing	cell phone and charger	blankets	candles	matches	whistle

GLOSSARY

bunker—a strong underground shelter

debris—the remains of something broken down or destroyed

Enhanced Fujita Scale—a system for measuring the strength of a tornado based on its wind speed and how much damage it causes

meteorologists—scientists who study and predict the weather

mobile homes—trailers that are used as houses at a permanent site

radar—a device that sends out radio waves and maps their reflections; radar helps meteorologists predict the weather.

siren—a device that makes a loud noise to warn people about something

Tornado Alley—an area in the central United States with a high number of tornadoes each year; Tornado Alley covers an area from Texas to South Dakota.

AT THE LIBRARY

Kostigen, Thomas. *Extreme Weather: Surviving Tornadoes, Sandstorms, Hailstorms, Blizzards, Hurricanes, and More!* Washington, D.C.: National Geographic, 2014.

Tarshis, Lauren. *I Survived True Stories: Five Epic Disasters.* New York, N.Y.: Scholastic Inc., 2014.

Ventura, Marne. *How to Survive a Tornado.* Mankato, Minn.: Child's World, 2015.

ON THE WEB

Learning more about surviving a tornado is as easy as 1, 2, 3.

1. Go to www.factsurfer.com.

2. Enter "survive a tornado" into the search box.

3. Click the "Surf" button and you will see a list of related web sites.

With factsurfer.com, finding more information is just a click away.

INDEX